PIANO · VOCAL · GUITAR

THE KINKS
GREATEST HITS

Cover photo: London Features archive

ISBN 978-0-634-03580-7

HAL•LEONARD®
CORPORATION
7777 W. BLUEMOUND RD. P.O. BOX 13819 MILWAUKEE, WI 53213

Visit Hal Leonard Online at
www.halleonard.com

THE KINKS

ALL DAY AND ALL OF THE NIGHT

Words and Music by
RAY DAVIES

Spoken: Oh, get 'em all out.

Guitar solo ad lib.

D.S. al Coda

DON'T FORGET TO DANCE

Words and Music by
RAY DAVIES

no, no, ___ no. For-get it for a while.

You

close.

Don't for - get to dance,

no, no, ___ no. Don't for - get to dance.

APE MAN

Words and Music by
RAY DAVIES

walk-ing 'round like flies man. __ So I'm no bet - ter than the an - i - mals sit - ting in their

cag - es in the zoo man. __ 'Cause com - pared to the flow - ers and the birds and the trees

I am an ape man. I think I'm so ed - u - ca - ted and I'm so civ - i - lized, 'cause I'm a
(Spoken:) In man's evolution he has created

strict veg - e - tar - i - an __ and with the o - ver-pop - u - la - tion and in - fla - tion and star - va - tion, and the
the cities and the motor traffic rumble, *but give me half a chance and I'd be taking off my*

ape man.

'Cause com- pared to the sun that sits __ in the sky, __ com-
I look out the win-dow, but I can't see the sky, __ 'cause

pared to the clouds as they __ roll by, __ com-pared to the bugs and the spi-ders and flies __
air pol-lu- tion is a- fog-ging up my eyes, I want to get out __ of this cit- y a- live __ and

I am an ape man. }
make like an ape man. }

La la la __ la la __ la la __

1.
la la __ la la.

2.
la la __ la la. __ Come on __ and love __

COME DANCING

Words and Music by
RAY DAVIES

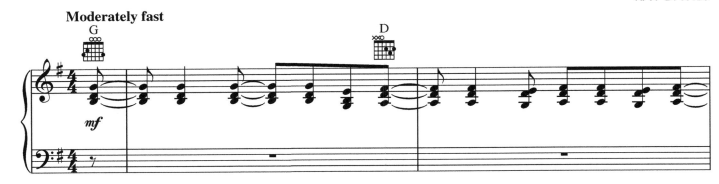

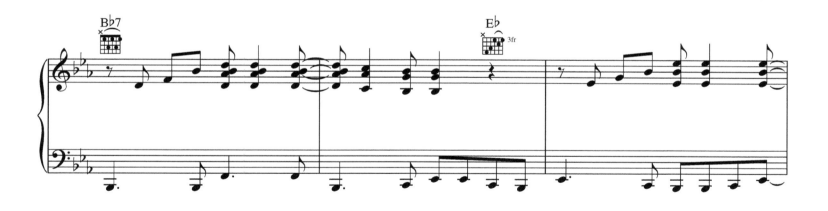

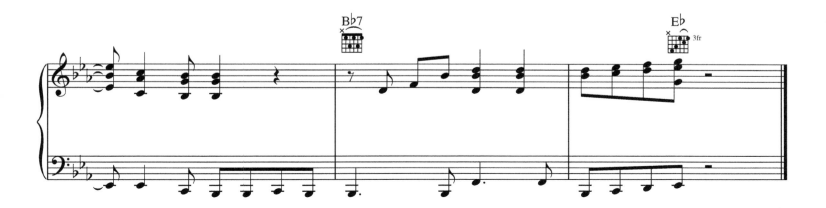

LOLA

Words and Music by
RAY DAVIES

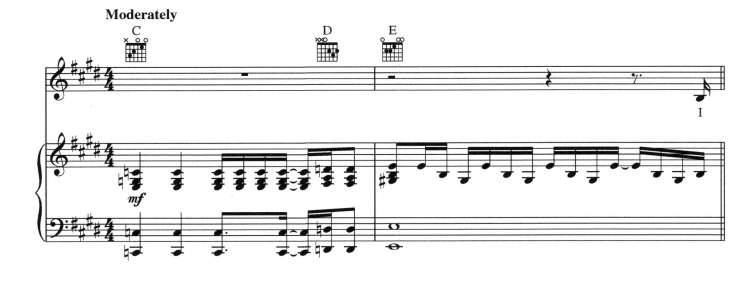

met her in a club down in old So-ho __ where   you drink cham-pagne   and it tastes just like __ cher-ry
I'm __ not the world's most phy-si-cal guy, __ but when she squeezed me   tight she near-ly broke my spine. __ Oh my,

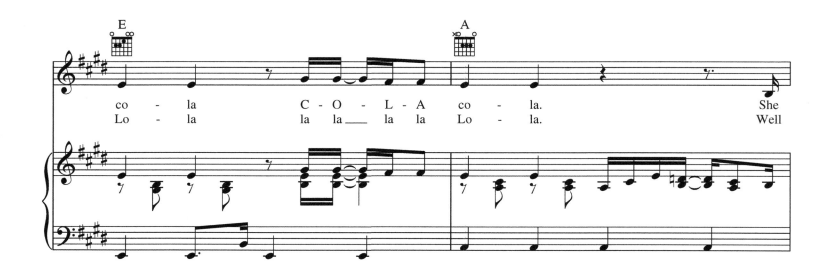

co - la   C-O-L-A   co-la.   She
Lo - la   la la __ la la   Lo - la.   Well

walked up to me and she asked me to dance._ I asked her her name and in a dark brown voice_ she said,
I'm not_dumb, but I can't un-der-stand_ why she walked like a wom-an and talked like a man. Oh my,

"Lo - la L - O - L - A Lo - la la la__ la la
Lo - la la la__ la la Lo - la la la__ la la

Lo - la."
Lo - la.

Well,

Well, we

ROCK 'N ROLL FANTASY

Words and Music by
RAY DAVIES

know ____ it's a mir - a - cle we ____ still go. ____ For all we know, ____
know, ____ we might still have a way ____ to go. ____ Be - fore you go, ____
know. ____ I feel free and I won't let go. ____ Be - fore you go, ____

____ we might still have a way ____ to go. ____
____ there's some - thing you ought ____ to know. ____
____ there's some - thing you ought ____ to know. ____

Hel - lo, me. ____ There's a

guy in my block. He lives for rock; ___ he plays rec - ords day and night. ___
Dan is a fan, and he lives for our mu - sic. It's the on - ly thing that gets him by. ___

SEE MY FRIENDS

Words and Music by
RAY DAVIES

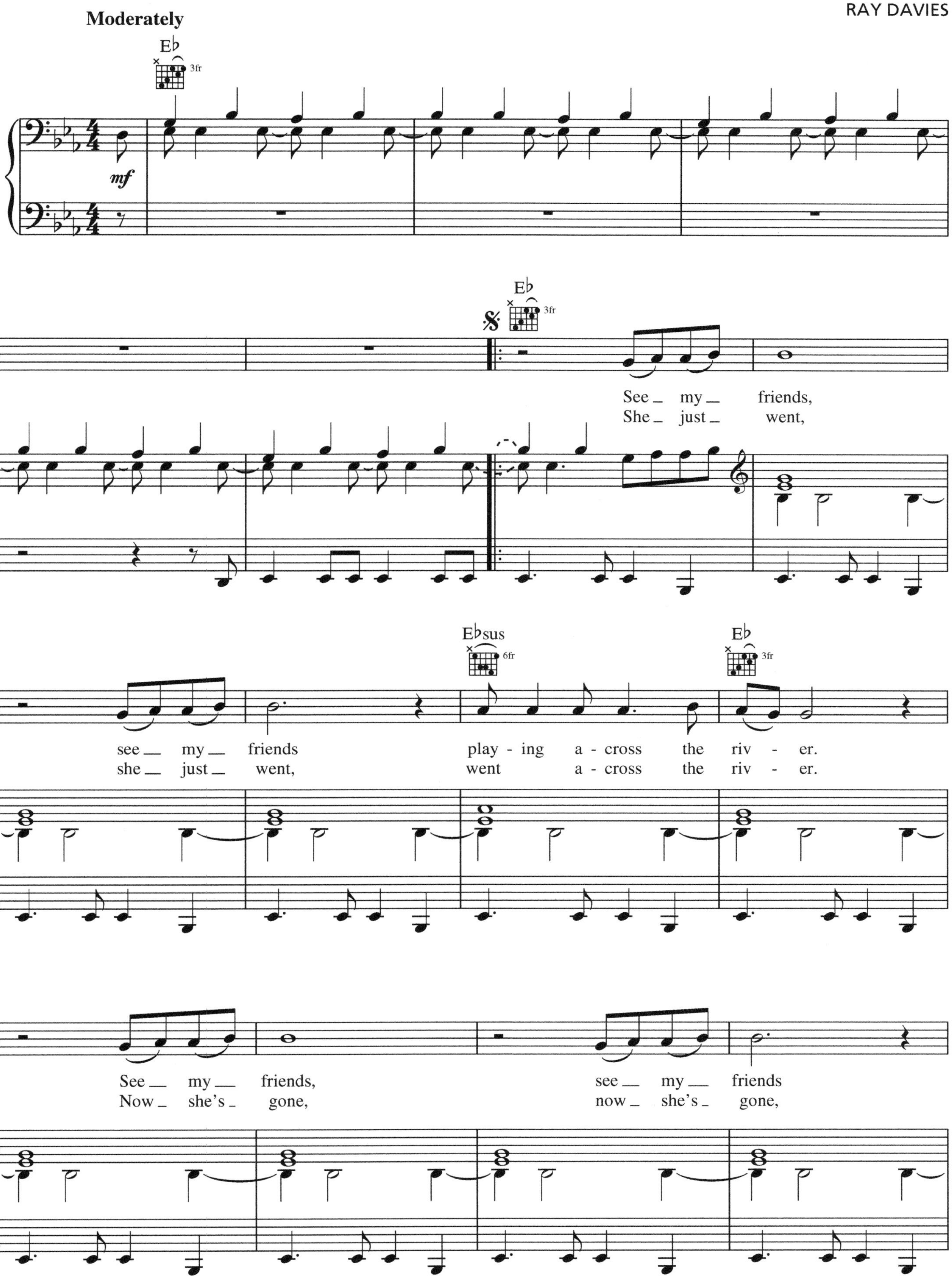

Moderately
E♭
3fr
mf
E♭
3fr
See my friends,
She just went,
see my friends playing across the river.
she just went, went across the river.
E♭sus
6fr
E♭
3fr
See my friends,
Now she's gone,
see my friends
now she's gone,

SET ME FREE

Words and Music by
RAY DAVIES

SLEEPWALKER

Words and Music by
RAY DAVIES

Moderately fast Rock beat

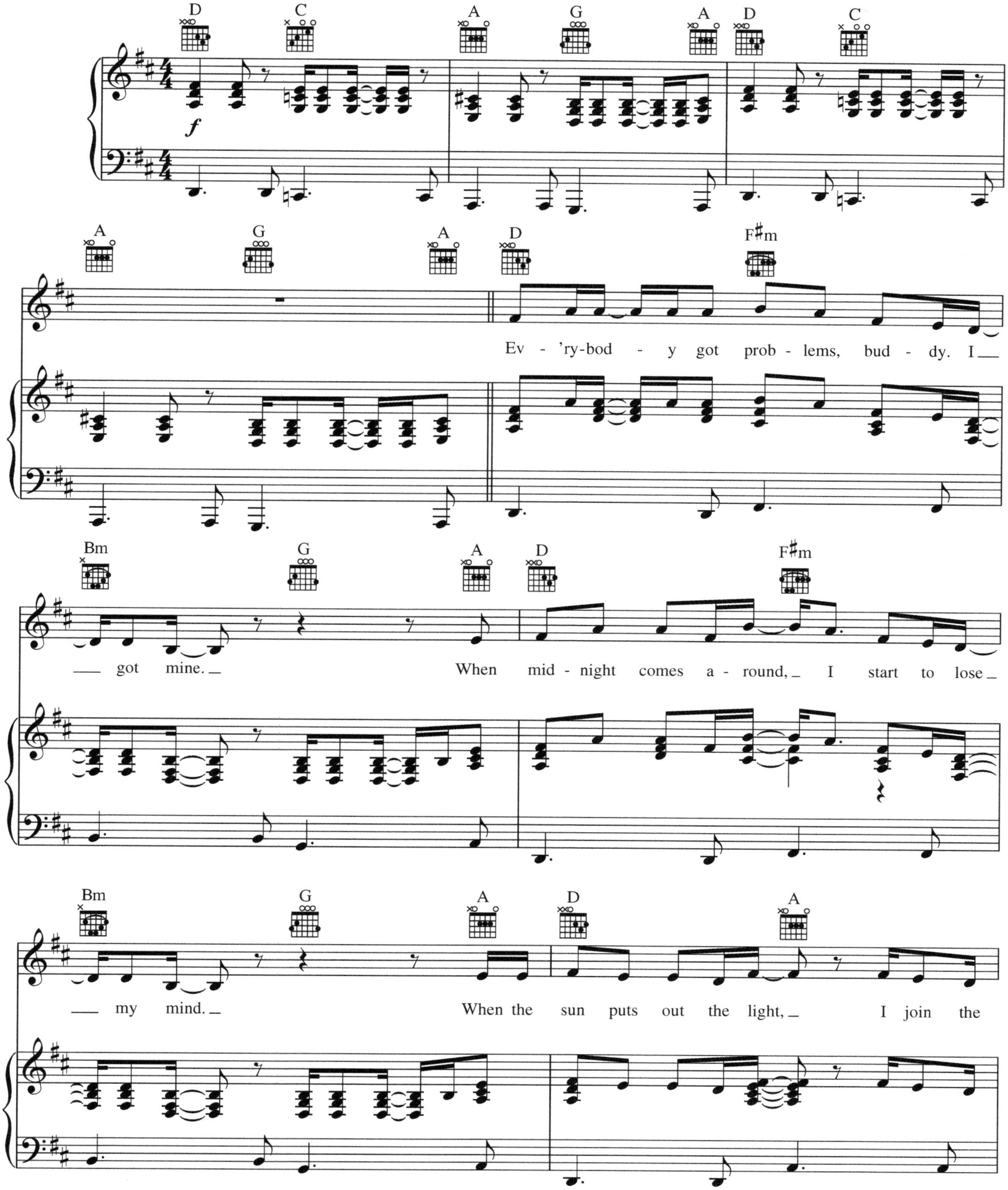

D C A G A D C
A G A D F♯m
Ev - 'ry-bod - y got prob - lems, bud - dy. I
Bm G A D F♯m
got mine. When mid - night comes a - round, I start to lose
Bm G A D A
my mind. When the sun puts out the light, I join the

prowl a - round __ when you're fast a - sleep. __ I walk a - round __ on my tip - py toes, __ and I

get in - to plac - es that no - bod - y knows. __ I'm al - ways a - round if you wan - na meet. __ You can

find me on al - most ev - 'ry street. __ You'll al - ways get __ me on the tel - e - phone. __ I'll e - ven

come to your home if you're ev - er a - lone. __

SUNNY AFTERNOON

Words and Music by
RAY DAVIES

(So)
TIRED OF WAITING FOR YOU

Words and Music by
RAY DAVIES

WATERLOO SUNSET

Words and Music by
RAY DAVIES

WHO'LL BE THE NEXT IN LINE

Words and Music by
RAY DAVIES

YOU REALLY GOT ME

Words and Music by
RAY DAVIES

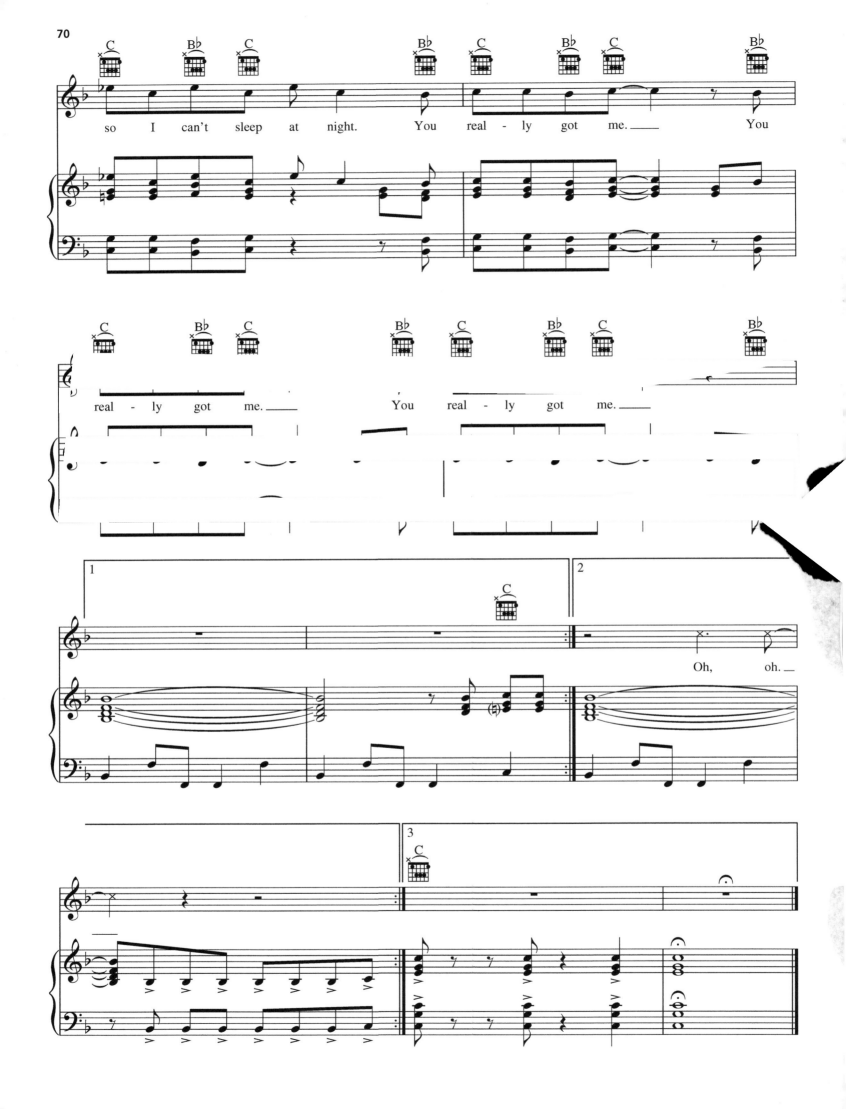

so I can't sleep at night. You real - ly got me. _____ You

real - ly got me. _____ You real - ly got me. _____

Oh, oh. _____